WHO MOVED MY STANDARDS?

*Joyful Teaching in
an Age of Change:
A SOAR-ing Tale*

MICHAEL D. TOTH

WHO MOVED MY STANDARDS?

Joyful Teaching in an Age of Change: A SOAR-ing Tale

With Tracy Bollinger, Betsy Carter, Carla Moore, and Terry Morgan

Illustrations by
Steve Asbell, with Isamar Jaquez

Learning SciencesInternational
LEARNING AND PERFORMANCE MANAGEMENT

1400 Centrepark Blvd, Suite 1000
West Palm Beach, FL 33401
717-845-6300

email: pub@learningsciences.com
learningsciences.com

Printed in the United States of America

21 20 19 18 17 16   2 3 4 5 6

MIX
Paper from
responsible sources
FSC® C013483

Library of Congress Control Number: 2016935665

Publisher's Cataloging-in-Publication Data
provided by Five Rainbows Cataloging Services

Names: Toth, Michael.
Title: Who moved my standards? / Michael Toth.
Description: West Palm Beach, FL : Learning Sciences, 2016.
Identifiers: ISBN 978-1-943920-03-7 (pbk.)
Subjects: LCSH: Education—Standards—United States. |
    Educational tests and measurements—United States. |
    Teacher effectiveness. | Academic achievement. |
    BISAC: EDUCATION / Professional Development. |
    EDUCATION / Evaluation & Assessment.
Classification: LCC LB3051 .T64 2016 (print) | LCC
LB3051 (ebook) | DDC 371.26--dc23.

This book is dedicated to the hardworking teachers everywhere who give of themselves so their little squirrels and birds can soar to higher standards.

Preface: Get Ready to SOAR

A SOAR-ing Tale is a parable about the challenges of change.

The characters in our tale, a group of blue jays and flying squirrels with some important lessons to teach their little ones, face a large-scale change. We show how, as teachers, we *can* learn to thrive in an environment where change is inevitable and to demonstrate how change very often spurs great leaps in growth and learning, great moves toward full potential.

The introduction of new standards has complicated things for teachers. These new standards, the most rigorous we've ever seen, have to be pulled apart, digested, deeply processed, and carefully applied in the classroom.

Most teachers do believe that new, more rigorous standards are a necessary step in the evolution of K–12 education, given the pressures of the new global economy. But faced with the difficulty of putting new standards into successful practice, much less getting kids to mastery, teachers may feel a bit overwhelmed as they search for the best ways to teach students the skills they so desperately need in this changing world. Those skills include the ability to think creatively, deeply, critically, analytically, and imaginatively; to think independently; and to work effectively with others. They demand both analytical (cognitive) and emotional (conative) skills.

Large, irreversible changes that shake the foundations of our cherished beliefs and close-held habits are often called "second-order change." Second-order change is the change from which there is no turning back. Such change often asks us to relinquish, or let go of, ideas that we have valued and that have worked for us in the past.

Our tale also illustrates how resilience in the face of change can light a path to new opportunities in learning and successes that may have been unimaginable. Teachers and students can reimagine their classroom environments to succeed in the new economy—equipping students with the necessary skills to collaborate and problem-solve success-fully. With the right kind of support, students can take increased responsibility, become much more autonomous, and draw on creativity and critical thinking to manage and push their own learning to new heights.

Such changes can be worth every bit of the struggle. Once we embrace the mindset that allows us to see our own potential shimmering in the dis-tance, our students can all learn to soar.

From the very top of the tree.

—Michael Toth

A Soaring Tale

The sun rose bright and hot over the forest. In a pine tree lived a family of flying squirrels and a family of blue jays. The little ones played together and were the best of friends.

Every spring, a new group of little flying squirrels and blue jays entered flying school. They learned to fly from the safety of their pine tree, over a dangerous stream, to land in a nut tree that was very close by. The nut tree was full of delicious and nutritious food for the long winter.

Each successive class had glided or flown to reach the nearby nut tree. The flight instructors taught their little ones the same way they had been taught by their own mothers and fathers and their grandmothers and grandfathers, generation after generation.

It was a good enough way.

This is how they did it.

The flight teachers organized the little ones into rows. They taught them the basics of jumping. They taught them to flap. They taught them to glide. Then the students practiced, jumping from branch to branch in the pine tree, each branch a bit farther away.

The little ones glided or flapped wildly with their still-forming wings. They each reached their branch separately. Some of the smaller or weaker ones barely made it. As long as they made it somehow, that was enough.

But then one night . . .

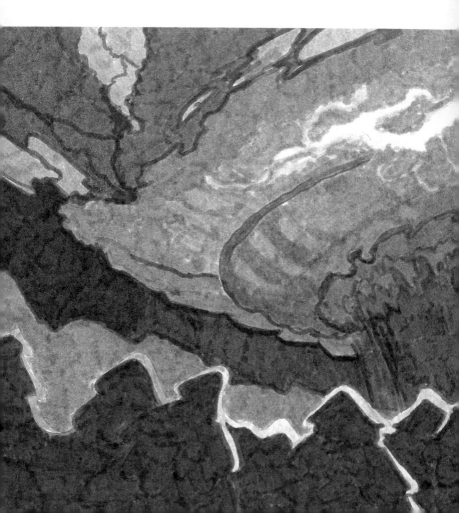

The wind began to blow. The thunder crashed. It was the worst storm they had ever seen.

Lightning struck the nut tree in the meadow, and with a terrible crackle and groan, it toppled to the ground.

When the animals woke and surveyed their world, they saw their familiar nut tree was gone. And worse, the next nut tree was much, much farther away. It was across treacherous terrain, where foxes and weasels roamed night and day.

What to do? What to do?

"We have never taught our little ones to fly so far," said the squirrel to the blue jay.

"Never so far on their own," agreed the blue jay. "Not in any generation."

At first, the flying school instructors tried teaching harder and harder. They gave the kids extra tasks. *Jump more! Jump higher!* The little ones leaped and flapped until they were exhausted. They could hardly chirp or chatter at the end of the day. School was no fun. And while there was some improvement, all the little ones were still not skilled enough to get to that faraway nut tree.

"Sometimes this feels impossible," the blue jay said nervously.

"Agreed," said the squirrel. "Teaching flight was hard enough in the old days."

"I'm exhausted and so are the kids," said the blue jay.

"Me, too," said the squirrel. "But we can't let our kids down. We just need to find a better way."

But they could already feel the sharp nip of winter in the air.

The flight instructors saw that it was a new world. Even the little ones could see it. Everything had changed.

They couldn't just give up, could they? *We must prepare! We must prepare!*

"I wish our world had not changed," the little ones chirped and chattered.

"If only . . ." the blue jay thought.

The flight instructors saw that flapping and jumping harder would be no help. Their old way of practicing would *never* get all the students to the distant nut tree in time, no matter how hard they tried.

So the teachers met to come up with a new plan.

To get to that distant nut tree, the little ones would need to build new skills, they decided. They would need to go far beyond just flapping and gliding practice.

They skillfully laid out the tasks at hand.

The little ones would need to know geography and the physics of flight. They would have to know how to judge wind velocity and direction. And most important, they would have to learn the sequence for their flight path.

- "We can recognize/recall vocabulary: *thrust, drag, lift, weight, Newton's first law.*"

- "We can analyze the principles of flight and explain how they work together or in combination in various weather conditions."

- "We can work in a team to apply the principles of flight to practice, and adjust our practice as necessary to soar farther until we reach the new nut tree."

The students would have to learn to work as a team to fly farther than any class had before. All the students must soar together. Not one could fail or fall.

"How will we ever teach the little ones so much, so fast?" the squirrel and the blue jay asked each other.

The flight instructors met as a teacher team and talked and talked. At last, they came to an agreement. To learn so many new skills before winter, the little ones would simply have to work together.

"None of us is as smart as *all* of us," said the squirrel.

"Sticks in a bundle are unbreakable," said the blue jay.

Yes, the little ones would need to work as a team to figure out how to get to that distant nut tree. Not even one child could be allowed to fail, or fall into the jaws of the predators prowling below.

At first, the little ones worried and complained. They were used to the flight instructors always telling them what to learn and how to learn.

How could they succeed at this impossible task?

"It's a new world," the blue jay told his chicks. "You must be quick and agile. You must be perceptive and thoughtful."

"In our new world, there will always be problems to solve. You must be able to do this for yourselves," said the squirrel to her little ones. She anxiously hoped they were up to the task.

"We can help you learn the skills you need, but we can't possibly be there to help you fly forever."

The little ones tried this way and that way.

They practiced circling once around their home pine tree, using all the principles of flight but never straying too far.

When they had mastered some skills, the flight instructors encouraged them to push a little farther. They circled their pine tree twice.

And then three times. And so on and so forth.

This was fun! The little ones were thinking and practicing on their own. The stronger, faster kids helped the smaller, weaker ones, encouraging them and offering tips from what they had discovered. Each student had a role to play, although those roles changed. Even when they made mistakes and learned from them, it was exciting.

The teachers saw that the students were helping each other. The squirrel and the blue jay exchanged looks of secret pride. "I guess we can step back and let them do it on their own," the squirrel whispered.

"Just let them soar a little farther each time," the blue jay agreed.

But the little ones still hadn't figured out how to fly far enough to reach even the nearest pine tree. The flight instructors watched, a little anxiously, and waited.

If the instructors had to swoop in when the kids veered too far off course, they made sure to ask questions to help the little ones figure out how to improve. "The learning *must* belong to the little ones," they said to each other.

Nobody would fail. Nobody would fall.

But still, the cold wind of coming winter ruffled
their feathers and nipped at their paws.

Then one day, the littlest flying squirrel said, "I wish I had wings and could fly!"

Eureka! The little ones tried something they had never tried before. They paired up. The flying squirrels glided as far as they could with the little blue jays holding tight and flapping on their backs to keep them aloft.

Round and round the pine tree, until they were quite sure they were ready.

And then, on to the nearest pine tree.

And on to the next one.

Their instructors encouraged them all, even the littlest and timid ones. They asked good questions. They supported them to stretch. They let the students take more and more responsibility. And they celebrated everyone's accomplishments.

Until at last the little ones reached the distant nut tree.

And what do you think they saw when they got there?

They sat in the high branches and looked out at a whole new forest of nut trees that they had never seen before.

They saw that they could certainly reach all those trees if they worked together.

"Our new world has no limits!" they said to each other.

And through the long winter, as they soared from tree to tree together, not a single child was lost. Not even one.

They all **SOARED** together!

The End

Teaching for the New Economy

Change will lead to insight far more often than insight will lead to change.

—Milton Erickson

You probably realized while you were reading our *SOAR-ing Tale* that the faraway nut tree is not just your average nut tree. When the old nut tree the blue jays and flying squirrels depended on is struck by lightning, the flying instructors realize they have to get their little ones a lot farther along to be successful. As a teacher or principal, you may have come to a similar realization when you first encountered new academic standards. But that nut tree in the distance represents more than new standards: it's also a symbol of the changing world we're preparing our students to enter.

All that flapping and leaping from branch to branch in the same tree, all that direct instruction, seem inadequate and artificial when the flying instructors are faced with that nut tree so far away. They realize immediately that their world has changed. And they come to the realization that their instructional methods have to change too.

As a teacher or school administrator, you're most likely struggling with some of the same issues. Our traditional model of lesson planning and instruction is no longer adequate for the challenges of meeting new standards or for success in the new economy, and here's why.

The old economy classroom was "manufacturing-centric." This model had its purpose when manufacturing jobs were plentiful. The classroom learning environment was good at producing the skills workers needed for mass production or assembly-line jobs.

So what did the old economy classroom look like? You may recognize it, because it still persists in many schools.

Domains of knowledge and skills were taught in isolation—science class had no connection to

English, math no connection to art. Students were directed regarding what to do and when to do it. Order and efficiency were prized. Students learned the subtle soft skills for this era: how to conform, to be orderly, to receive instruction, to accurately restate facts, to speak when called upon by someone in authority, to refrain from talking to other students during instruction. If students *did* try to work with other students to solve a problem, the teacher often corrected them to do their own work. Such skills were necessary in an assembly line or production workplace, where supervisors instructed workers to do isolated repetitive tasks accurately and without variance. Most of us learned in environments just like this one. It's the model of learning still operating at some level in many classrooms.

Today, due to globalization and technology, the "do as directed" repetitive task jobs have largely been automated or sent overseas. So the soft skills, or interpersonal skills, needed for today's new economy are *very* different. The higher-wage jobs of the new economy require dynamic teaming. Employees may serve on one or more teams formed specifically to resolve an issue or create a solution.

In dynamic teaming, team leadership may shift. You may pick the team, or the team may pick you based on your skills and strengths. Exhibiting leadership, of your own and others' work, even when you are not "the boss" is a prized skill in the more informal, flatter, and constantly shifting organization. Employees take ownership of their work and their teams' results. They analyze information and issues, learn from their failures, and come up with better solutions. They challenge ideas to spur even better ideas.

Employees need interpersonal skills for success in this new economy, where they are often confronted with challenging projects that require fluid and complex problem solving, persistence in the face of difficult tasks, and less direction from superiors. Today's higher-wage positions require the ability to research, analyze, and synthesize information into persuasive arguments or compelling presentations. Employees' jobs may depend on their ability to master the facts, come up with solutions, and win others over with their ideas.

Sound familiar? It was just these challenges our squirrels and blue jays had to face, just these skills they needed to develop, when their nearby nut tree was struck by lightning.

New state standards were developed precisely to reflect the demands of today's world and to foster the skills for success in the new economy. Do our classrooms today reflect this? *It makes little sense to teach academic standards developed for a new economy in a classroom learning environment that reflects the old economy.* To develop these skills in our students, we'll have to go well beyond simply adding one-to-one technology to traditional classrooms. The shift we're describing is far less about technology and much more about transforming the way students *experience their learning.*

How can we transform our classroom learning environments to reflect the new economy and not the old? Teachers who make this transition in their classrooms are skilled at forming and facilitating student academic teams, where kids wrestle with the content as applied to real-world scenarios, where their thinking and problem-solving skills are fully engaged, and where the teacher expertly moves to the background to facilitate and guide when learning goes off track. After the foundational knowledge and skills have been laid, teachers adeptly transition to applying that knowledge and those skills to engaging real-world scenarios for students. When classrooms make this transition, both teachers and students are able to master the full intent and rigor of new standards.

The following chart helps make sense of how the old economy classroom environment differs from the new.

Old Economy Classroom Environment	New Economy Classroom Environment
Teacher is doing most of the "work."	Students are doing most of the "work."
Teacher is doing most of the talking and directing.	Students are doing most of the talking and are directing their own work.
Teacher feels like she/he is pushing the students to learn.	Students take ownership of their academic progress and pull toward their learning goals.
Students have a hard time visualizing how the learning will help them in the real world.	Students are seeing the connections to the real world through their work.
Teacher feels the pressure to engage and hold students' attention.	Students are highly engaged in complex tasks and real-world problems.
Teachers feel fatigue and the pressure to cover content.	Students are feeling mentally stretched but excited about the task and what they are discovering.

Through this process, students begin to think like scientists, poets, mathematicians, and historians. They can make choices, work in diverse teams, and apply content to real-world problems. There are huge benefits for both teachers and students when classrooms are transformed this way. Teachers find that their jobs get easier because students are shouldering some of the responsibility for their own learning. By focusing on priority standards instead of attempting to cover everything as an equal priority, teachers have more time for planning deep lessons. When teachers are monitoring for learning in the moment, they can place less emphasis on creating and grading quizzes, homework, and weekly tests. Teachers can identify and support struggling students while the rest of the class is engaged in team work.

Is this shift realistic for all students? We would answer, unequivocally, *yes*. We have personally witnessed, in schools where we have supported them through this process, inclusion classrooms where less advantaged students are immersed in highly interactive student teams, where peer coaching is taking place, and where children are practicing verbal and social skills. When we have seen one student struggle, their peers have provided the emotional and academic support the student needs. When the academic team is functioning at a high level, students of all abilities flourish. With the right supports and adaptations, disabled or disadvantaged students have blossomed as they worked on real-world, complex problems with the encouragement of their peers. We have seen kindergarten children using the academic vocabulary and thinking skills of much higher grades. And we have seen excitement and challenge return to classrooms where the light has long been dimmed.

Students are ready for a new learning environment that has these attributes. Think about how our students experience the new economy in their out-of-school lives. They engage in 24/7 wired communities, where they form teams to game together, coordinating their efforts with complex strategies to reach higher levels. They log into social networks, where they create and share content and videos and receive instant feedback through "likes," followers, and friend requests. Then what happens when they go to school? Students report they have to "power down" and feel as though they've traveled back in time. They're expected to sit quietly, memorize facts and figures that they could easily google, work in isolation, and practice, practice, practice. If teachers are finding it hard to hold students' attention, no wonder. The real world is out there, competing with our every move.

Just as the little squirrels and birds were not successful on their first attempts, neither will your students likely be. Failed attempts to get your students to soar are not the same as failure. Real failure happens only when we stop before we reach our goal. In fact, failing is inherent in complex learning. As Indian scientist Dr. Abdul Kalam so famously wrote, "If you fail, never give up because F.A.I.L. means 'First Attempt in Learning.'" We must try new methods to get our students to soar, and not all those attempts will succeed. We (and our students) will learn and adjust until it works. This is the process of mastery.

Changing our classrooms to reflect the world of today and tomorrow certainly requires an investment of effort. But once students become engaged in the real-world complex tasks and are eager to reach learning goals for themselves and their teams, it will pay off for the rest of our teaching careers.

The good news is that students are coming to us prewired for this transformed new economy classroom learning environment.

We just have to tap into it.

Some Final Thoughts

Here are a few foundational concepts to help you transform your classroom learning environment.

- Students can't be direct-instructed into becoming critical thinkers. Students develop critical-thinking skills by working with a level of autonomy from the teacher while applying the learned content to complex tasks in real-world scenarios.

- Teacher over-support can rob students of the autonomy necessary to develop critical-thinking and teamwork skills. Focus on scaffolding the release of responsibility to the students for their own learning. If students are on task but struggling with content, allow them to practice persistence and stretch themselves mentally. If they have misconceptions, errors in reasoning, or gaps in understanding that are preventing progress in the complex performance task, they may not yet be ready for the complexity of the task. Clear up misunderstandings and content gaps and try again.

- All learning in classrooms should be based on the academic standards, with thoughtful planning to align performance tasks, success criteria, and levels of deeper thinking with the standards. The standards-aligned learning goal should always be clear to students, so they can track their own progress to mastery.

- Not all standards are equal. Work with your curriculum office to identify the power standards and the supporting standards.

- Student academic teams need well-developed roles and expectations, including team leaders, common performance tasks but accountable individual work, and visible peer coaching. The team is only successful if *all* team members are successful. If it feels like you are pushing the team to learn, then you do not yet have a student learning team.

- When designing real-world-scenario performance tasks, think like a scientist, musician, engineer, movie producer, or author. You will want your students to begin to take on these roles through the performance task design.

- As students perform real-world complex tasks, make sure they use correct academic vocabulary and engage in discussions and thinking like student scientists, engineers, mathematicians, essayists, or historians. They should be questioning each other's claims, probing reasoning, and examining text evidence as they investigate and solve problems or create new solutions.

- Most important of all, have fun with it. If you as a teacher are not feeling creative and excited about the performance task, it's not likely your students will be either. If you're having fun teaching it, they most likely will have fun learning it.

The resource pages of this book include a powerful tool for examining student evidence. Use the SOAR (Students' Opportunities for Achieving Rigor) Rubric to gauge your progress as you transform your classroom learning environment.

Our goal in writing this book, and in the many classroom visits and consultations we have done across the United States, is to return the joy and creativity to teaching, a joy that so many teachers have told us they hunger for. As you equip students with the skills they need to flourish in the new economy and the future workforce, we know you'll find that you are truly *soaring* together.

Resources

Visit **www.learningsciences.com/SOAR** for more resources to help your students soar to higher standards.

SOAR (Students' Opportunities to Achieve Rigor) Rubric

The SOAR Rubric is a companion tool to standards-based lesson plans. It will help you ensure that students are achieving mastery of the standards within the context of new economy skills and real-world applications.

Teachers may use the rubric to gauge if their classroom learning environment is making progress toward new economy skills and culture through the student evidence described in the SOAR Rubric. The SOAR Rubric is a student evidence rubric, *not* a teacher observation rubric; the rubric shifts the focus from teacher to students. Teachers should have the freedom to be creative in trying different techniques, while checking the student evidences on the SOAR Rubric to see which techniques are working. Getting all students to *SOAR* is the goal. Have fun with the process. As your students *SOAR*, you will feel positive energy increase in your classroom as students become more actively engaged and own their learning.

Student Evidences	Traditional (Old Economy)	Student Centered	Real-World Applied (New Economy)
		Student Groups	
Student Grouping	Whole class or clustered into small groups doing independent work	Groups working on a common task	Teams working to solve or accomplish a real-world applied task
Group Task Taxonomy Level	Recall and skill/concept[1]	Application of skill/concept[1]	Extending knowledge through strategic, analytical, and visionary thinking[1]
Student Discussions	Talks mostly when prompted by teacher	Talks unprompted to other students about the content, common task, or group process; limited use of academic vocabulary	Talks using academic vocabulary with meaning and understanding, questions other students' thinking or claims, cites text evidence for own thinking or claims, probes other students' thinking and claims, takes various positions on a subject to examine its merits

continued →

Student Evidences	Traditional (Old Economy)	Student Centered	Real-World Applied (New Economy)
Taxonomy Level of Student Discussions	Recall and skill/concept[1]	Application of skill/concept[1]	Extending knowledge through strategic, analytical, and visionary thinking[1]
Student Group Dynamic	Whole class but little small-group dynamic	Functions with low autonomy, roles often unclear, awkwardness and uneven effort among group members	Team roles and norms are clear, all members engaged in discussions and tasks, peer coaching is evident, members question each other and examine claims, members encourage each other and recognize effort and progress
Student Accountability			
Definition of Success	Students are often unable to identify what success is or looks like other than a grade	Definition of success is provided for the performance task by the teacher and known by the students	Students are involved in determining what success is and looks like for performance tasks aligned to rigorous standards

Student Evidences	Traditional (Old Economy)	Student Centered	Real-World Applied (New Economy)
Peer Accountability for Learning	Little to no peer accountability	Limited peer accountability for their role in the group, most accountability coming through the teacher	Team is only successful if all team members reach their goals, members hold each other accountable for achieving the team and individual learning goals with peer support visible, teams self-regulate behavior to optimize learning
Students Tracking Their Own Progress	Students rarely track their own progress to academic goals	Students are tracking their progress to academic goals	Students have a role in determining their own academic goals and tracking their progress to those goals aligned to rigorous standards
Tracking of Team Progress	Little to no tracking of group progress to academic goal	Teacher tracks the group progress to academic goal	Team tracks its own progress to the academic goal
Practical Application			
External Real-World Application	Passive glimpse of the real world through images, videos, lecture-based examples	Performance tasks reflect a real- or future-world scenario and authentic resources	Students help design the performance task with the real- or future-world scenario and authentic resources

continued →

Student Evidences	Traditional (Old Economy)	Student Centered	Real-World Applied (New Economy)
Use of Technology	Technology predominately augments lecture such as interactive whiteboards and student-response devices or students using computer-aided interventions or learning programs	Technology used to retrieve facts and definitions or automate traditional functions like taking notes and writing a paper using word-processing software	Technology used to investigate, explore, create, analyze, and connect the classroom to real-world experiences
Self-Actualization[2]	Low self-actualization due to lack of choice, limited work with peers, lack of empowerment, lack of feelings of accomplishment through effort and contribution to something greater than self	Moderate self-actualization through working with peers on shared tasks and collaboration with limited autonomy during group work	High self-actualization through ability to make choices, empowerment to drive one's own learning, accomplishment through reaching individual and team goals through persistence and effort, making a meaningful and valuable contribution to something greater than oneself through helping others achieve their goals, celebrating team successes, and continuous improvement

[1] Webb's Depth of Knowledge

[2] Self-actualization: the achievement of one's full potential through creativity, independence, spontaneity, and a grasp of the real world (Dictionary.com, http://dictionary.reference.com/browse/self-actualization)

Explanation of the SOAR Rubric

The Traditional (Old Economy) column is typically dominated by direct instruction or lecture and independent practice. It is often how new teachers learn to control their classrooms. The teacher is the center of the stage and the predominant voice that is heard. The classroom feels orderly, quiet, and well managed. The students are compliant. This is an environment conducive for delivering content through lecture. The energy and pacing in the classroom is primarily dependent upon the teacher.

The Student Centered column is the necessary middle step on the way to the new-economy learning environment. The gradual release of responsibility ensures the teacher never loses control of the classroom through this transition step to the new economy learning environment. In the Student Centered column, the classroom is noisier and students are engaged with their peers in small groups, typically processing and elaborating on content that was previously delivered through direct instruction. The teacher may design a lesson that toggles between the direct instruction of the Traditional column and the Student Centered activities in the second column, such as processing and elaborating activities in groups. Typically, in the Student Centered column we see students working in groups as an extension of a traditional lesson.

The Real-World Applied (New Economy) column is the classroom learning environment in which students and teachers can thrive and feel energized. These classrooms have students avidly engaged in content through complex real-world tasks as students take on the roles of scientists, biographers, engineers, and authors. The teacher has skillfully released responsibility by granting autonomy and choice in the learning. Autonomy and choice help foster ownership and responsibility. Classroom norms evolve so that students respectfully challenge each other's claims citing evidence in order to help peers who are struggling to understand and to ensure accuracy and correctness of all team products. Students use academic vocabulary in discussions about the content and tasks. In this setting, students begin to feel empowered to take on more learning and greater roles in the team and to co-own the norms so they learn to self-regulate in a more dynamic environment. Misbehavior that is rooted in boredom and lack of academic challenge tends to be significantly diminished when students are highly engaged in this new learning environment.

There is a big difference between students working in groups and students working in teams. When a teacher forms a group, the teacher typically decides the task and the pacing, and provides support. The group functions with low autonomy from the teacher. Many of us remember the dreaded occasional "group work" assignment where the "smart" kids did most of the work and the rest of the group shared the grade. When students form into a high-functioning learning team, the dynamic is very different. Roles are clear, and team members take pride and ownership in their work and the performance of their team. They learn how to work smarter each team cycle, and their rate of learning increases. When one team member struggles, the others help. The team owns the success of everyone on the team. There is a constant informal peer-coaching process going on as the group discovers and fails, and then tries again. Lively debate and even passionate arguments over content and discoveries take place. The teacher skillfully roams the room, not interrupting the learning but ensuring conversations focus on the task and reminding students, if necessary, of the norms. Passion is encouraged, coupled with respect.

Using the SOAR Rubric

A useful place to start with the SOAR Rubric is to privately and honestly reflect on your classroom learning environment. In which column do you find the preponderance of student evidences? What you find is neither good nor bad. You are simply taking stock of your starting point, which allows you to begin charting your journey. Having evidences in various columns is normal. The goal is to shift the preponderance of evidences, over time, toward the New Economy column. The benefit of that shift is truly enormous to you and your students.

We have helped many schools and classrooms make this full shift across the country in our Demonstration Schools for Rigor and Demonstration Classrooms initiative. The shift did not happen overnight. Not every lesson went as it was planned. But when teachers work as a team with a purpose, there is nothing they cannot overcome.

In every case, at the end of that journey, teachers told us the joy of teaching had returned, that students were actually better behaved, and that teaching got easier as students took more responsibility for their own learning and the learning of their peers.

You can start with selecting a few evidences from the rubric to "soar an activity" or "soar a lesson." Bring your learnings into your teacher team and help others begin to soar their lessons and learn from each other. Move up to working as a teacher team to soar a week of lessons and support each other through discoveries and successes. In a short while, you and your students will be soaring higher and farther than you ever imagined. (Visit learning sciences.com/SOAR for resources to help your little squirrels and birds soar to higher standards.)

Tips

A teacher team, for example, may decide to examine one of the following tips per meeting or, more ambitiously, take one week of lessons in common and spiral through the tips as a collaborative team, planning, teaching, and examining student evidences with the SOAR Rubric. The teacher team will learn from failures and successes and then encourage one another to try again. It is not a race; it is a process of continuous improvement guided by student evidence.

Tips for Planning Standards-Based Lesson Sequences

1. Start with standards-based planning for a sequence of lessons by identifying the priority and supporting standards for what you are going to teach.

2. Unpack the standards to identify the academic vocabulary, foundational and more advanced concepts, and taxonomy level of thinking students need to exhibit with the more advanced concepts.

3. Plan to teach the academic vocabulary, foundational concepts, and then more advanced concepts using complex texts and a method of checking to determine if the students have correctly grasped these concepts and vocabulary. This approach allows for a scaffolding of knowledge

and skills across the lesson sequence with increasingly rigorous thinking tasks for students. Also use the SOAR Rubric of student evidence to guide the creation of tasks that will foster a new economy learning environment.

4. Plan a performance task where students will work in teams to apply the more advanced concepts using correct academic vocabulary in a real-world-scenario problem. The task should require deeper thinking, complex problem solving, and connections to other knowledge domains. Student teams will need to investigate, cite text evidence to support their claims, take positions, and present their solutions while other student teams critically review the work to see if it achieves success criteria that embody the full intent and rigor of the standards.

Tips for Teaching Standards-Based Lesson Sequences

1. Check with students to ensure that learning targets for each lesson are clear to

them and that the conceptual connections to prior learning are made.

2. As the learning progresses, have students self-check their work against the standards and also the level of thinking they need to exhibit in the work. Then have peers recheck to confirm the work is ready for the teacher's inspection. This gives students the opportunity to own their learning and practice peer coaching.

3. Keep the SOAR Rubric at your side, monitoring the classroom environment for student evidences of the new economy skills as students master the rigor of the academic standards.

4. Enjoy yourself and have fun with the students as they take on more responsibility for their learning and progressively demonstrate new economy skills. Remember, learning from failure is inherent in complex learning. Allow yourself and your students the freedom to fail on your pathway to SOARing.

About the Authors

 **Michael D. Toth** is founder and chief executive officer of Learning Sciences International. Formerly the president of the National Center for the Profession of Teaching and a university faculty grant director, Toth transformed his university research and development team into a company that is focused on leadership and teacher professional growth and instructional effectiveness correlated to student achievement gains.

Toth is actively involved in research and development, gives public presentations, and advises education leaders on issues of leadership and teacher effectiveness, school improvement, and professional development systems. He is coauthor, with Robert J. Marzano, of *Teacher Evaluation That Makes a Difference: A New Model for Teacher Growth and Student Achievement* (ASCD), and he is coauthor of *School Leadership for Results: Shifting the Focus of Leader Evaluation* (LSI).

Tracy Bollinger's twenty years in education as a  dynamic classroom teacher and knowledgeable instructional leader led to her career as a staff developer with Learning Sciences International. Ms. Bollinger has been part of school improvement planning, curriculum writing, district-wide professional development, and instructional coaching in Pennsylvania districts. Student achievement and teacher growth are her passion and areas of focus, as she works with demonstration schools in Florida and coaching academies across the nation.

Betsy Carter, PhD, is a seasoned educator with  thirty-five years of experience as a teacher and K–12 administrator. Her teaching experience includes classrooms K–5 and math at the middle school and high school levels. She has a strong passion for teacher effectiveness and student success. Dr. Carter received her doctorate in organizational leadership from Miami University of Ohio, where she also served as a visiting assistant professor in the teacher education department. In her current position, Dr. Carter has worked as a staff developer, content developer, and in research and development.

Carla Moore, MSEd, an experienced profes-sional developer, teacher, and administrator, oversees professional development and product development for Learning Sciences International, with a special emphasis on teacher and administrator effectiveness. She is nationally recognized for her commitment to K–12 education, having received the 2013 Florida Association of Staff Development Award, the Schlechty Centre Conference Fellowship, and the Treasure Coast News Lifetime Achiever of Education Award, among others. She is coauthor with Dr. Robert J. Marzano of *Creating & Using Learning Targets & Performance Scales: How Teachers Make Better Instructional Decisions.*

Terry Morgan is dedicated to clarity and transparency in teacher growth and believes that when teachers are empowered to improve their practice, the result is significant impact on student achievement. He coaches and motivates educators to provide both clarity in pedagogy and the structure and supports necessary for teachers to succeed. Mr. Morgan served as a high school math and physical education teacher in Iowa and Florida. He was also a district-based staff developer for the St. Lucie County Schools in Florida and was instrumental in leading the implementation of the Marzano instructional framework. Now with Learning Sciences International, his current focus is coaching teachers to establish the necessary shifts to impact every child.

About the Illustrators

Steve Asbell has illustrated for clients such as La Tourangelle, Ferry Morse Seed, and Bonnie Plants, and is now beginning his foray into children's and educational illustration. He is also the author of *Plant by Numbers* (Cool Springs Press) and the creator of the blog *The Rainforest Garden* (featured in *Southern Living* magazine), and he regularly writes for Tuesday Morning, Yahoo, *Florida Gardening* magazine, Zillow, and Burpee Seed Company. When he isn't having a blast drawing or writing, Steve loves to cook and garden with his young son and apprentice.

Isamar Jaquez was born and raised in South Florida after her parents moved to the United States from the Dominican Republic. She is a senior at Alexander W. Dreyfoos School of the Arts, where she specializes in drawing and storytelling. She says she has been doing commissions for her artwork since ninth grade, and her artistic influences include Disney and Studio Ghibli. Jaquez will graduate from Dreyfoos in 2016, and she plans to pursue a career in the arts after college as an illustrator, comic artist, or animator. Her hobbies include cooking pancakes, making stuffed animals, sleeping, and interpreting dreams.

Dreyfoos School of the Arts participates in the Learning Sciences Demonstration Schools Initiative.

About Learning Sciences International

Learning Sciences International provides research-based professional development, customized initiatives, personalized e-learning, on-site training, research services, and books on effective pedagogy to teachers, leaders, schools, and districts.

As education professionals, we are interested in one thing only: helping educators deepen student learning through their own growth and development.

Student achievement is directly linked to teacher effectiveness. With powerful, standards-driven instructional strategies, leadership coaching, and formative assessment techniques, educators and leaders get a clear picture of the impact they have and what they need to do to help all students succeed in today's increasingly demanding learning environment.

Visit us at LearningSciences.com.

Notes